CW01151584

Original title:
Dreary Twinkles Inside the Faerie Bead

Copyright © 2025 Swan Charm
All rights reserved.

Author: Linda Leevike
ISBN HARDBACK: 978-1-80559-494-9
ISBN PAPERBACK: 978-1-80559-993-7

Spheres of Hope in Solitary Night

In the quiet of the night, so deep,
Stars whisper secrets, softly they leap.
Each twinkle a promise, a dream that may soar,
In the shadows of silence, I long for more.

Shadows dance lightly, the moon casts a glow,
Guiding my thoughts where the brave hearts go.
In solitude's embrace, I find my release,
A flicker of hope, a moment of peace.

The cold breeze carries the whispers of fate,
Each breath a reminder, it's never too late.
The night wraps around me, a comforting shroud,
As I gaze at the heavens, lost in the crowd.

Spheres of bright futures in the dark align,
With each pulse of starlight, my spirit will shine.
In the tapestry woven from dreams and from fears,
I gather my courage, dissolving my tears.

As dawn's early light breaks the solemn deep hue,
I rise with the sun, like the blooms that renew.
The night held my worries, but hope held me tight,
In the spheres of the cosmos, I found my own light.

The Sorrowful Whisper of Wandering Lights

In the night, whispers drift low,
A dance of stars, in sorrow's glow.
Flickering faint, as shadows creep,
They weave their tales while others sleep.

Each light a wish, a hope forlorn,
Lost in the vastness, silently torn.
Softly they mourn, a distant call,
Guiding the dreamers, one and all.

Through the dark, they flicker and fade,
Echoes of laughter, a memory made.
Longing for warmth, the heart beats slow,
In this vast void, they bravely glow.

With every twinkle, a promise shared,
Yet, in their journey, each is scared.
A celestial path, they bravely tread,
In the sorrowful night, with dreams ahead.

Dim Radiance in the Garden of Shadows

In the garden where twilight lies,
Soft blooms whisper under darkened skies.
Faint outlines dance in the cool night air,
Secrets linger, hidden with care.

Moonlight drapes on petals worn,
A fragile glow where dreams are born.
Each shadow holds tales of old,
In whispers of hues both faint and bold.

Winds carry scents of warmth and loss,
Echoes of love that sometimes cross.
Silent stories in the dim embrace,
A haven of solace, a sacred space.

In this twilight realm, hearts intertwine,
With every flicker, a moment divine.
They dance in secrets, both shy and profound,
In the depths of night, where hopes are found.

Silken Echoes of a Faded Dream

Once, in the silence of endless skies,
A dream was woven, with truth and lies.
Silken threads spun with laughter's grace,
Now linger in shadows, a tender trace.

Whispers of glory, once bright and clear,
Faded, they tremble, as night draws near.
Crumbled hopes on a timeworn bed,
Rest in the silence, where dreams are led.

Through golden dawns, now grayed with age,
Stories unfold in a turning page.
Echoes of moments, so sweet, so true,
Drift through the air, both old and new.

Yet in the silence, a spark ignites,
Reviving the warmth of forgotten nights.
Dancing on air, the whispers beam,
In the soft glow of a fading dream.

Orb-shaped Sorrows in Starlight

In the quiet dusk, sorrows take shape,
Round like the moons, their fragile drape.
In starlight's glow, they twist and weave,
Wonders of grief that few can believe.

Each shimmer holds a tear's embrace,
Reflecting loss in a delicate space.
Yet, in their flight, they seek the dawn,
Yearning for warmth as shadows yawn.

With every pulse of celestial light,
They tell of battles and lonely nights.
Orbiting hopes, like jewels in the sky,
Drawing forth dreams that refuse to die.

In the vastness, we find our way,
Each orb-shaped sorrow, a beacon to stay.
Together in darkness, we charge and rise,
Bathed in the glow of starlit skies.

Fragments of Luminous Melancholy

In the quiet of twilight's fade,
Whispers of dreams in shadows laid.
Soft echoes of laughter start to part,
Holding the remnants close to heart.

Glimmers of hope in the pale moon's glow,
Drifting like leaves in a soft, warm flow.
Thoughts like fragments of broken glass,
Reflecting faces of moments past.

Each sigh a note in the dusk's embrace,
Carried on winds in this timeless space.
Yearning for light in the fading hues,
Clinging to memories, gentle and bruised.

Words unspoken linger in the air,
Lingering feelings, a sweet despair.
As stars awaken, they bless the night,
In fragile dreams, we find our light.

Though time may steal what our hearts hold dear,
In the soft shimmer, we persevere.
Fragments of joy in the depths of gray,
Softly illuminating our way.

Shadows Breathing in a Whispering Dawn

Morning spills softly, a tender grace,
Shadows retreating, finding their place.
Whispers of night fade into the light,
Breathing in warmth, dispelling the fright.

Rustling leaves sing a delicate tune,
Awakening flowers, adorned in dew.
The world stretches wide, ready to bloom,
In shadows of dawn, dispelling the gloom.

Echoes of dreams linger in the air,
Murmurs of hope twine with sunlit prayer.
Each ray a promise, each gust a sigh,
Painting the canvas of a brightening sky.

Time dances lightly, from night to day,
Shadows breathing in soft shades of gray.
Every heartbeat whispers, "Here we belong,"
In the cradle of dawn, where we are strong.

Nature awakens, a symphony played,
In vibrant hues, the darkness betrayed.
As shadows retreat from the sun's embrace,
We find our rhythm in this sacred space.

Fading Gleams in an Unseen Grove

In the heart of the grove, where silence weaves,
Fading gleams dance on the autumn leaves.
Sunlight trickles through branches entwined,
Holding the secrets that nature has lined.

Here dreams take root in the soft, rich earth,
Whispers of stories, a place of rebirth.
Each rustle is magic, a soft lullaby,
Lifting the spirits to the azure sky.

Shadows cradle the remnants of light,
Fading into the arms of the night.
Every sigh of the wind, a caress,
Wrapping the grove in harmonious dress.

Time drips slowly like honey from trees,
Moments abiding, carried on the breeze.
In this unseen haven, we find our peace,
As fading gleams offer a sweet release.

So linger anew where the shadows play,
Embrace the stillness, let worries sway.
In the fading light, we find our own way,
In an unseen grove, forever we stay.

The Enchantment of Dimming Lights

As day retreats, the sky starts to gleam,
In shadows and whispers, we weave a dream.
Lights dim gently, a soft, tender glow,
Embracing the night with a warmth we know.

Stars flicker softly like thoughts drifting by,
Painting the canvas of the deepening sky.
Each moment holds magic, a story to share,
In the enchantment of night, we breathe the air.

With every heartbeat, the world quiets down,
In the dimming light, we wear love's crown.
Voices of twilight sing sweet lullabies,
Wrapping us softly in their tender ties.

As echoes of daylight slip into dreams,
We gather the stardust from shimmering streams.
In the enchantment of dimming lights, we find,
A place where our spirits and hopes are entwined.

So dance with the shadows, embrace the night,
In each fading flicker, there's warmth, there's light.
The enchantment unfolds as our hearts take flight,
In the tender solace of dimming light.

Shadows of Enchanted Orbs

In twilight's grasp, the shadows play,
With whispers soft, they drift away.
Orbs of light in silence gleam,
Casting spells like a woven dream.

In the forest where secrets hide,
The glowing spheres, they dare to glide.
Among the trees, they dance and swirl,
Unraveling tales of the night's unfurl.

Each orb a story, a fading sigh,
Reflecting stars from the midnight sky.
In their embrace, the lost find home,
Guided by light, no need to roam.

Forgotten paths in the dusky haze,
Illuminate hearts in a gentle blaze.
Through the shadows, a journey unfolds,
In enchanted night, all magic holds.

With every flicker, a tale reborn,
In the hush where dreams are worn.
Together they weave the night's adorn,
Eclipsing fears until the dawn.

Whispers of Twilight Reflections

As daylight bows to night's caress,
Whispers flicker, an old success.
Reflections dance on water's edge,
Seductive secrets, they pledge.

In hushed tones, the stars collide,
Time dissolves like a fleeting tide.
With every glance, a memory's spark,
Illuminates the dreams, once dark.

Twilight hues in soft embrace,
A fleeting beauty, a gentle trace.
In the silence, shadows creep,
While the world around gently sleeps.

Bound by the night, souls intertwine,
Lost in moments, so divine.
In whispers sweet, the truth is found,
In twilight's heart, we're forever bound.

Each reflection holds a tale to share,
Of love and loss, of pain laid bare.
In every glow, a fleeting chance,
To find the light in the dark's romance.

Glistening Sorrows in a Mystic Sphere

Glistening tears in a mystic sphere,
Hold the sorrows we often fear.
Of dreams unmade, and paths untread,
Whispers of what lies ahead.

In shadows deep, where echoes call,
A lumined hope breaks through the fall.
Each droplet holds a wish, a prayer,
For the lost love that lingers there.

The mystic sphere spins tales of old,
Of fleeting moments, stories told.
In each glimmer, a haunting sigh,
That ebbs and flows like the tide's reply.

Sorrows painted in vibrant hues,
In twilight's light, they softly muse.
With every shimmer, the pain recedes,
Embracing life as a heart concedes.

In this sphere, all fears dissolve,
As glistening sorrows find resolve.
Release the weight, let spirits soar,
In the embrace of the evermore.

Luminescent Echoes of Forgotten Dreams

In the stillness, echoes bloom,
Luminescent whispers chase the gloom.
Forgotten dreams rise from the deep,
Awakening stories long lost in sleep.

With every glow, a vision shines,
As heartbeats weave through shadowed lines.
In the night, the past returns,
Lighting the soul where passion burns.

Echoes of laughter, sighs of pain,
In luminescent forms, they remain.
Each flicker tells of joy and strife,
The dance of memories, the pulse of life.

Through the shadows, echoes flow,
A tapestry of all we know.
In every corner, a dream may gleam,
Inviting us back to where we beam.

Lost but not gone, they softly gleam,
In the quiet, find solace in dream.
With luminescent echoes, we reclaim,
The forgotten paths that call our name.

Ghostly Sparks in the Hidden Grove

In shadows where the whispers dwell,
Soft echoes weave their silent spell.
A flicker glints through leaves of night,
These ghostly sparks dance out of sight.

They twinkle low, in twilight's breath,
Embers of dreams that flirt with death.
A phantom's laugh, a rustle near,
In the hidden grove, all things appear.

Beneath the boughs, a tale unfolds,
Of secrets kept and hearts of gold.
The moonlight bathes the forest floor,
Where spirits linger, longing for more.

With every step, the past awakes,
In vibrant hues, the silence quakes.
A journey lost from time's embrace,
Yet ghostly sparks find their own place.

In the stillness, memories glide,
Through ancient roots, where shadows hide.
A mingling of the real and dream,
In the hidden grove, all's not as it seems.

Luminous Grief in a World Apart

A heart that aches beneath the weight,
In solitude, we contemplate.
Each tear a star that falls from grace,
Luminous grief, an eternal trace.

In twilight's glow, we find our peace,
Yet echoes of loss refuse release.
A silent song that haunts the night,
In shadows cast by fading light.

The world moves on, but we remain,
In memories laced with joy and pain.
An absent smile, a gentle sigh,
A lingering warmth that will not die.

We walk the line of hope and fear,
In spaces where your voice rings clear.
A flicker lights the path ahead,
Yet darkness wraps the heart in dread.

In dreams, we touch what we can't keep,
In the quiet depths, our sorrows seep.
Luminous grief, a tender art,
In a world apart, you hold my heart.

Dim Stars Through Enchanted Veils

Through veils of mist, the starlight weaves,
A tapestry of hope and leaves.
They shimmer soft, those whispers old,
In dim-lit skies, their tales unfold.

The night dons shades of velvet blue,
While wonders wait for hearts so true.
Each twinkling light, a distant dream,
In the hush of night, the shadows gleam.

Secrets lie in every glint,
A magic lost, a fleeting hint.
With every breath the universe sighs,
As dim stars blink, and silence cries.

Beneath the canopy of grace,
We search for warmth in the cold space.
The enchanted veils, they softly part,
Revealing truths that touch the heart.

In midnight's arms, we find our way,
Through dim stars' songs that softly play.
A cosmic dance, a timeless call,
With enchanted veils, we rise and fall.

Shimmering Pathways of Broken Wishes

In the quiet dusk, the dreams take flight,
Shimmering pathways in the fading light.
Each wish we cast, a fragile thing,
In the tapestry of hope we cling.

With every twist, a journey bends,
The past's embrace, a tale that mends.
Through winding trails, we wander far,
With broken wishes, we reach for stars.

In echoes lost, the heart still beats,
Where time concedes to bittersweet.
Every step we take reveals the scars,
On shimmering pathways, we chase our stars.

Yet in the dark, the light can spark,
A flicker bold against the stark.
In woven realms of what may be,
We'll find our strength, forever free.

Through broken wishes, dreams arise,
In shimmering pathways, the spirit flies.
With hope as guide, we'll chase the dawn,
Together forever, our fears are gone.

Ethereal Murmurs Among Silent Grove

Whispers linger in the breeze,
Between the leaves, a soft sighs tease.
Shadows dance where dreams entwine,
In the grove where stars align.

The moonlight kisses tender ground,
In hush of night, no other sound.
Silence sings a haunting tune,
Crickets play beneath the moon.

Ancient trees with wisdom deep,
Guard the secrets that they keep.
Each bark a tale, each branch a song,
In this sacred space where I belong.

A tapestry of twinkling light,
Guides the wanderer through the night.
In stillness, echoes softly call,
Inviting souls that chance to fall.

Ethereal murmurs fill the air,
As spirits weave without a care.
In the grove, where shadows blend,
Life and death forever mend.

Glittering Ghosts of Forgotten Paths

Along the trails where memories sleep,
Glittering hues of secrets seep.
Each step echoes with wishes past,
In this realm where dreams are cast.

Moonbeams dance on cobbled stones,
Whispers of the lost and lone.
Each path a story, each turn a tale,
Guide the heart where shadows sail.

Ghostly laughter fills the night,
In the midst of fading light.
Footprints linger, softly fade,
In the dreams that time has made.

Rustling leaves tell of days gone by,
Beneath the vast, embracing sky.
Glittering remnants softly weave,
A tapestry we dare believe.

Yet in the twilight's gentle hush,
Forgotten paths make the heart rush.
In each glimmer, truths arise,
As ghosts beckon 'neath the skies.

Veils of Dusk, Secrets of Dawn

Dusk wraps the world in soft embrace,
Cloaked in shadows, time finds its pace.
Whispers of twilight kiss the ground,
In this magic where dreams abound.

Stars ignite in a velvet sky,
A silent nod as night draws nigh.
The world exhales, a gentle sigh,
As mysteries weave and moments lie.

Beneath the veils of fading light,
Secrets stir, waiting for flight.
Each heartbeat echoes in the night,
As day drifts softly out of sight.

With dawn's first blush, a light is born,
Revealing paths where shadows worn.
The sun breaks forth, a golden crown,
In the embrace of night, once drowned.

In radiant hues, the world awakes,
As nature's dance ignites and shakes.
Veils of dusk, secrets of dawn,
In flow of time, our souls are drawn.

The Last Light of a Fading Realm

In twilight's grip, shadows conspire,
The last light flickers, a fading fire.
Once vibrant hues now dimmed and pale,
As silence weaves its delicate veil.

Faint echoes bounce off crumbling stone,
Whispers of places once brightly shone.
Time's gentle hand tugs at the seams,
Of a world built upon fleeting dreams.

Through tangled roots, secrets flow,
In this fading realm, dreams still glow.
Haunting beauty, fragile and rare,
Fading light, yet we still dare.

As dusk unfolds its velvet shroud,
We gather strength, united and proud.
For in the depths of night we find,
The strength of spirit, beautifully intertwined.

The last light whispers of what once was,
In shadows twirling, a fading buzz.
Yet even in dusk, hope still gleams bright,
In the heart of the dark, we search for the light.

Cerulean Hues of a Forgotten Night

In whispers low, the stars reside,
Beneath the moon, where dreams abide.
Cerulean skies paint tales of old,
In shadows cast, our secrets told.

The night's embrace, a soft caress,
Wrapped in silence, we confess.
With every breath, the past ignites,
Cerulean hues of forgotten nights.

A distant echo calls your name,
In twilight's grasp, we're not the same.
The nightingale sings, a haunting tune,
Under the spell of the silvery moon.

Lost in thoughts, we wander wide,
Through memory's lanes, we will glide.
With hearts entwined, we take our flight,
In cerulean dreams of the night.

As dawn approaches, colors blend,
The night's allure begins to end.
Yet in our souls, the blue remains,
A tapestry woven with love's refrains.

Luminous Crystals of Haunting Beauty

In gardens rare, the crystals gleam,
Shimmering softly, a mystic dream.
They catch the light in amber frames,
Whispering secrets, ancient names.

With each dawn's rise, they dance anew,
In radiant shades of piercing blue.
Their luminous glow, a siren's call,
Echoes through shadows, enchanting all.

Beneath the surface, time does wend,
In silent depths where stories blend.
The crystals hold the art of grace,
Reflecting beauty in every face.

Yet fleeting is their sacred light,
As dusk approaches, they take flight.
Within our hearts, they leave a trace,
Luminous memories in time's embrace.

The haunting beauty lingers near,
In every sigh, in every tear.
Through life's odd paths, we find our way,
With luminous crystals guiding the day.

Flickering Footfalls on Twilit Paths

As daylight wanes, the shadows grow,
Flickering footfalls guide us slow.
Through twilight's grace, we roam the night,
In hushed whispers, hidden from sight.

This winding trail, where dreams converge,
Murmurs of tales begin to surge.
Each step reveals the truth untold,
In twilight's glow, the heart is bold.

The moon above bathes us in light,
A lantern bright on our shared flight.
With every echo, memories spark,
Flickering footfalls through the dark.

Through rustling leaves and quiet streams,
We chase the echoes of our dreams.
In the canvas of night, we find our part,
With flickering footfalls, we shape the heart.

As the stars awaken one by one,
We walk the path until it's done.
Hand in hand, we'll face the morrow,
With flickering steps, conquering sorrow.

The Dance of Shadowed Fragments

In corners dim, where shadows meet,
Fragments of past begin to fleet.
The dance of silhouettes, we see,
Echoes of what is yet to be.

With grace they twirl, in moonlit haze,
Waltzing through forgotten days.
Each fleeting glance, a story spun,
In shadowed fragments, we are one.

Their rhythm speaks in silent tones,
Revealing heartbeats in hushed moans.
A tapestry woven of light and dark,
The dance ignites an unseen spark.

As twilight deepens, shadows blend,
In this embrace, the night descends.
We lose ourselves in time's sweet trance,
The dance persists, a timeless chance.

So take my hand, we'll drift and sway,
Through shadowed realms, we'll find our way.
In fragments lost, we find our grace,
The dance of life, in every space.

Echoes of the Unseen Dreamscape

Whispers drift on twilight's breath,
Lost in the echoes of what lies beneath.
Shadows weave in a dance of grace,
Fleeting visions in a timeless space.

Stars align in a silent song,
Guiding wanderers where they belong.
Hues of memory bloom and fade,
In the warmth of dreams, we are unafraid.

Freed from the confines of waking thought,
Each shimmering fragment, gently caught.
Time suspends in this mystic realm,
A tapestry woven, where hearts overwhelm.

Voices echo, soft as a sigh,
Carried away on the night's lullaby.
With every heartbeat, the landscape swirls,
A whirlpool of magic in celestial pearls.

In the hush of night, we find our way,
Among the stars, forever we'll stay.
Every whisper a promise, every glance a kiss,
In the dreamscape's embrace, we find our bliss.

The Lament of Light's Soft Touch

Morning breaks with a gentle approach,
Casting shadows, a soothing reproach.
Colors melt in a golden hue,
Enveloping all in the warmth of you.

But as day fades, sorrow unfolds,
Whispers of twilight in secrets told.
Each ray a memory, tenderly pinned,
Lamenting the light that can no longer begin.

The breeze carries tales of the past,
Echoes of laughter, too sweet to last.
Softly it weaves through the weeping trees,
Cradling the dreams that are lost in the breeze.

Yet in this twilight, hope remains bright,
A promise of dawn in the heart of the night.
Silhouettes dance in the ebbing glow,
A testament to love, while shadows grow.

With every sunset, we learn to let go,
Of fleeting moments that cease to flow.
Each soft touch of light, a bittersweet boon,
Guides our spirits beneath the moon.

Faint Sparks in the Languid Air

In the stillness, whispers ignite,
Faint sparks flutter, a flicker of light.
Beneath the veil of a hazy sky,
Dreams trapped in amber, as moments fly.

Time lingers on, a warm embrace,
Each secret shared, a delicate trace.
Awake in silence, we feel the hum,
Of laughter and longing, sweetly begun.

A canvas of twilight, brushed in gold,
Stories unfold in the silence untold.
Gentle sighs ride the whispering breeze,
As shadows sway among the trees.

Flickers of hope in the shadows play,
Guiding lost souls throughthe fray.
A beacon of warmth, bright yet discreet,
In the languid air where moments meet.

Each faint spark, a glimpse of the soul,
Binding our hearts, making us whole.
As dusk settles softly on the shore,
We inhale the magic, craving more.

Shards of Luminescence in Autumn's Embrace

Crimson leaves dance in the crisping air,
Whirling and twirling, free of all care.
In autumn's embrace, we find delight,
Shards of luminescence glowing bright.

Softly the sun drapes a golden sheen,
On amber fields where we've always been.
Time flows gently, like a winding stream,
In the heart of the season, we dare to dream.

With every gust, a laughter rings clear,
Filling the air as the harvest draws near.
Moments converge in a vivid display,
A tapestry woven in colors of gray.

In the twilight glow, shadows start to blend,
Embracing the season with each twist and bend.
Nature's canvas, a brilliant parade,
Of shards of luminescence, not to fade.

With every heartbeat, we cherish the sight,
Of autumn's beauty, a fleeting delight.
Time dances on, yet we hold it close,
In the embrace of the season, we rejoice the most.

Grains of Hope in a Clouded Sky

In shadows cast by doubt's embrace,
A flicker glows in silent space.
Each grain a wish, with dreams we sow,
A promise bright, through storms we go.

The clouds may gather, dark and deep,
Yet hope will rise where others weep.
With every drop, a heart will bloom,
As light breaks through the darkest gloom.

A journey starts with tiny seeds,
In barren lands, we plant our needs.
These grains of hope, so small, so grand,
Will change the face of this vast land.

We chase the dawn, the warmest light,
Through tempest's wail, we hold on tight.
For in the storm, our spirits grow,
With every grain, we learn to flow.

So let the clouds, they swirl and spin,
For grains of hope lie deep within.
With faith as our unwavering guide,
We face the storms and turn the tide.

Celestial Reflections in Still Waters

Beneath the surface, calm and clear,
The stars descend, their light held near.
Each ripple whispers tales of night,
In stillness found, the world ignites.

A mirror casts the sky on earth,
In tranquil depths, we find our worth.
The heavens dance, in water's hold,
Each glance revealing secrets told.

The moonlight spills like silver dreams,
In every wave, a story gleams.
With every breath, we touch the skies,
As magic glows in our soft sighs.

In quiet moments, hearts entwine,
Reflecting hopes where souls align.
The universe, in droplets bright,
Invites us all to share the light.

So gaze upon the waters still,
And ponder dreams that gently thrill.
For in their depths, we find our way,
Celestial paths in shades of gray.

The Melancholy of Shattered Stardust

Once gleaming bright, the stars did soar,
Now scattered fragments, lost in lore.
Each piece a wish, a longing sigh,
In silent nights, we ask the why.

The cosmos breathes a solemn tune,
As shadows dance 'neath the pale moon.
With every glance, a heart does break,
For stardust dreams, we yearn to wake.

In glimmers lost, we seek our past,
A fleeting glimpse that fades so fast.
These memories weave a tapestry,
Of love and loss, the stardust plea.

The echoes call, a haunting wail,
In every fragment, love's soft trail.
Yet in the sorrow, beauty lies,
As shattered hopes give rise to skies.

So gather pieces, one by one,
And find the light where dreams begun.
For in the ruin, there's a spark,
Of stories penned in shadows dark.

Glimmers of Solitude in Midnight Gardens

In gardens where the shadows play,
The moonlight weaves a dreamlike fray.
Each petal whispers tales of night,
In solitude, we find our light.

The stars unfurl, their soft embrace,
As night unfolds a sacred space.
In quiet moments, hearts take flight,
Through glimmers found in soft twilight.

Amidst the blooms, a calm resides,
Where solitude and peace abides.
With every breath, the world stands still,
A canvas waiting for our will.

The scent of jasmine fills the air,
In midnight's hush, we shed our care.
As dreams collide with whispered sighs,
In gardens lone, the spirit flies.

So wander deep where shadows dwell,
And listen close, for time will tell.
In solitude's sweet, tender hold,
The midnight gardens weave their gold.

Whispers of Silent Beads in the Night

In shadows deep, the whispers twine,
   Silent beads of dreams align.
The moonlight bends, a gentle guide,
   Where secrets of the heart reside.

A fleeting breeze, a tender sigh,
   Echoes soft beneath the sky.
Each glimmer speaks of tales untold,
   In silver threads of night, behold.

Embrace the stillness, let it weave,
   A tapestry of hopes, believe.
The starry lace in darkness sewn,
   A quiet pulse, the night has grown.

Whispers linger, time stands still,
   As moonlight dances, dreams fulfill.
In silent beads, the world draws near,
The night reveals what hearts hold dear.

With every breath, the stories bloom,
   In whispered tones dispelling gloom.
Soft echoes through the skies so bright,
   Whispers of silent beads in the night.

Gossamer Threads of Invisible Wishes

In the dawn's light, wishes soar,
Gossamer threads, forevermore.
Floating softly, delicate and shy,
Invisible dreams in the vast sky.

With each heartbeat, hope entwines,
Woven gently through the pines.
A wish upon the breeze takes flight,
Dancing softly in morning light.

Through lush meadows, secrets trace,
In silent whispers, they find their place.
Crafted softly in the dew,
Gossamer threads connect me and you.

Each shimmering strand, a story grand,
Held by time, with a gentle hand.
As daylight fades, wishes blend,
In twilight hues, a soft descend.

With hopes wrapped tight in woven dreams,
Invisible wishes burst at seams.
In every heartbeat, love persists,
Gossamer threads of our quiet wishes.

Flickering Memories in the Mist

In the morning haze, memories dance,
Flickering softly, a fleeting glance.
Veiled in mist, the past entwined,
Each moment glimmers, undefined.

The echoes call, familiar yet far,
Like distant lights, a guiding star.
Through sleepy woods, shadows play,
Flickering memories, lost in the day.

A gentle whisper drifts on breeze,
Capturing time with effortless ease.
Through layers deep, the heart recalls,
Flickering warmth where silence falls.

Softly the fog wraps round our fears,
Each flicker holds a thousand tears.
In the twilight glow, they intertwine,
Flickering memories, yours and mine.

As the sun rises, shadows fade,
Yet those moments are gently laid.
In the misty dawn, they find their way,
Flickering memories, in disarray.

The Gloomy Glow Between the Leaves

Beneath the boughs where shadows creep,
The gloomy glow invites to weep.
In whispers hushed, the twilight sighs,
A dance of light where darkness lies.

Through tangled branches, flickers gleam,
Soft echoes of a distant dream.
In quiet corners, secrets brew,
The gloomy glow reveals the true.

Like fireflies caught in twilight's hold,
Chasing warmth through the shadows cold.
Each flicker tells of tales forgotten,
In the gloom, new paths are begotten.

Softly the night wraps time in chains,
In every sorrow, a joy remains.
Between the leaves, the darkness sways,
The gloomy glow in twilight's haze.

With every breath, the shadows weave,
In haunting echoes, we believe.
The past and present, intertwined,
The gloomy glow, forever defined.

The Veiled Light of Dreaming Spirits

In twilight's embrace, whispers arise,
Phantoms dance softly, beneath darkened skies.
Veils of the night, secrets they keep,
Guiding lost dreams through the shadows so deep.

Flickering hopes in the silent starlight,
Each glow a tale of love, loss, and flight.
Beneath the moon's gaze, they gently weave,
Stories of hearts that yearn and believe.

Cloaked in the mist, where memories play,
Spirits converge as night turns to day.
A gentle reminder, in each sighing breeze,
That dreaming is endless, like the swaying trees.

In the hush of night, a soft refrain,
The echoes of laughter, the taste of pain.
Bound by the silks of ethereal streams,
These veiled light bearers carry our dreams.

So let them guide through the folds of your mind,
Where sorrows dissolve and peace you will find.
In the veiled light of the dreaming spirits,
A world of wonder, where our heart merits.

Twilit Sadness in a Realm of Whispers

In the fading light, shadows converge,
Silent sighs linger, their weight we urge.
Echoing softly, through the rustling trees,
Twilit sadness dances on the evening breeze.

Veils of the dusk hold stories untold,
Whispers of heartache begin to unfold.
As colors dim down, and night takes its flight,
We gather our sorrows, holding them tight.

Flickers of hope in the depths of despair,
Gentle reminders that life can be fair.
In this realm of whispers, we find our way,
Navigating shadows till the break of day.

Hushed tones of longing float through the air,
Cradling our hearts in moments so rare.
Twilit sadness wrapped in a tender embrace,
Revealing the beauty hidden in space.

So let us listen, as shadows converse,
In whispers of twilight, we find our verse.
A tapestry woven from sorrow and grace,
In this realm of whispers, we find our place.

Glum Lullabies Beneath the Glistening Canopy

Under the canopy, the stars wear a frown,
Where glum lullabies wrap the world in a gown.
Softly murmuring woes disguised as a song,
Echoing dreams where forgotten belong.

Beneath the glisten, shadows expand,
Whispers of sorrow brush against sand.
The night holds its breath, as we drift away,
Carried by lullabies into the fray.

A symphony played on the strings of the night,
Melancholy tunes that may bring us delight.
For in each lost note, a lesson remains,
Glum lullabies cradle our deepest pains.

Stars flicker dimly, as tears start to flow,
Holding our secrets, the night seems to know.
In this glistening realm, where shadows reside,
We gather our heartbeats, and let them collide.

So seek out the beauty beneath the despair,
In lullabies sung with a tender care.
For under the canopy, we learn to cope,
Finding solace in music, peace in our hope.

Ethereal Fables of the Weeping Wood

In the heart of the forest, where shadows kiss light,
Ethereal fables speak softly at night.
Trees weep gently, stories they share,
Of love lost and found, of burdens we bear.

Leaves rustle softly, a delicate sigh,
As whispers of legends drift through the sky.
Fables of wanderers seeking their way,
In the embrace of the woods, their spirits play.

Each tale unfolds in an echoing breeze,
Carried on currents that dance through the trees.
Thorns of past sorrows blend with the grace,
Of ethereal fables, time cannot erase.

In twilight's hush, the wood grows alive,
With tales of resilience that stir and revive.
Each heart becomes woven with threads of the past,
In the weeping wood, where dreams are amassed.

So listen attentively, hear their refrain,
For in every fable, there's fortune and pain.
In the solace of trees, our spirits can mend,
Ethereal fables, where journeys transcend.

Whispers of Diminished Light

In twilight's grasp, the shadows creep,
Soft murmurs dance where silence weeps.
Faded echoes drift on air,
Where once was brightness, now despair.

Faint glimmers trace the edges near,
A sighing breeze, a whispered tear.
Memories lost, like stars in flight,
Fade softly into the night.

Among the trees, the whispers share,
Secrets held in the cool night air.
Diminished flames of days gone by,
A fleeting glimpse, a quiet sigh.

In the hush, the world is bare,
Searching hearts find solace rare.
Within the void, a song so slight,
A fading warmth of diminished light.

Yet hope remains, a tender thread,
In every heart where dreams are fed.
For even in the deepest night,
A spark can stir, ignite the light.

A Flicker in Gloom

In the shroud of a heavy dusk,
Unseen shadows wear a mask.
A flicker stirs in the glum air,
Whispers promise, though dreams despair.

Eyes closed tight, we seek the flame,
Forgotten hopes call out by name.
Yet in the dark, one spark can bloom,
A flicker breaks the heavy gloom.

Beneath the weight of heavy skies,
Silent prayers in secret rise.
For every heart that learns to fight,
Will find its way back to the light.

Fading echoes of laughter ring,
A sudden hope, a timid spring.
In corners dark, new dreams resume,
A flicker found within the gloom.

So hold fast to that glint of gold,
Let weary souls find courage bold.
For from the depths, we rise anew,
With every flicker, life breaks through.

Shimmering Shadows of Forgotten Dreams

In twilight's haze, the shadows weave,
A tapestry of what we believe.
Shimmering threads of dreams once bright,
Now linger softly, lost in night.

Forgotten whispers haunt the air,
Echoes of hopes that disappear.
Yet every shadow holds a gleam,
A fleeting glimpse of what we dream.

Beneath the moon's pale, silver sigh,
Old fantasies begin to fly.
While memories fade, new paths align,
Shimmering softly, stars still shine.

In every heart, a silent quest,
To find the light that once was best.
Though shadows dance and dreams may scheme,
They shimmer still, those forgotten dreams.

So let them guide through endless dark,
Reviving flames, igniting sparks.
For in the night, we find our team,
In shimmering shadows of forgotten dreams.

Echoes of Wistful Glimmers

In the stillness where shadows play,
Wistful glimmers mark the way.
An echo whispers, soft and light,
Reminding us of lost delight.

Through tangled paths of ancient trees,
The haunting calls ride on the breeze.
Where laughter danced and joy took flight,
Now only echoes greet the night.

Yet in the quiet, dreams reside,
With glimmers faint, they still abide.
For every heart that dares to yearn,
Finds wistful glimmers in its turn.

As stardust falls on sleeping clay,
The echoes linger, never stray.
Though time can dim what once was bright,
Wistful glimmers spark the night.

So hold those echoes, soft, sincere,
Let them guide you, sweet and clear.
For in your heart, the light will burn,
With echoes of wistful glimmers to return.

Flecks of Forgotten Brilliance

In the quiet corners of the mind,
Flecks of light dance, soft and blind.
Memories linger in gentle sways,
Whispers of laughter from distant days.

Fading echoes, colors collide,
In shadows where dreams once tried.
Time's embrace, both tight and loose,
Caught in the beauty of its own ruse.

Fragments of joy, lost and found,
In the silence, they softly resound.
A glimmering past, forever near,
Fleeting moments that draw us here.

Through tangled vines of thought they weave,
Glimpses of what we so believed.
Light spills softly into the dark,
Flecks of brilliance, a hopeful spark.

In the chaos, a truth remains,
Hidden treasures in gentle pains.
For in the fading, we see the light,
Flecks of brilliance, shining bright.

Melodies Woven in Silvery Shadows

In twilight's grasp, soft tunes arise,
Melodies hush beneath the skies.
Echoes of whispers, sweet yet bold,
Stories of ages, gently told.

The silvered shadows dance and sway,
Carrying secrets of the day.
Notes entwined like threads of gold,
Unraveling dreams, both warm and cold.

Each hum, a heartbeat, soft and clear,
Reverberates in the quiet ear.
Harmony plays on the edge of night,
Melodies shimmer, a fleeting light.

In the depths, where silence sings,
A weaving tapestry timeless brings.
Together we drift, lost in the sound,
In shadows, our solace is found.

So linger here, within the embrace,
Of silvery shadows, find your space.
For in their depths, our souls align,
Melodies woven, a love divine.

Restless Glimmers Beneath the Overcast

Under a blanket of grayish skies,
Restless glimmers seek to arise.
Flickers of hope, like stars so bold,
Whispering secrets, stories untold.

The clouds may roll, heavy and deep,
But glimmers stir from their silent sleep.
Caught in the dance of shadows and light,
Yearning for dawn to conquer the night.

In stillness, each flicker tells a tale,
Of dreams deferred and wishes frail.
Beneath the weight, they flicker and shine,
Restless glimmers, a cherished sign.

As storms hover with thunderous roar,
Hope twinkles bright at the horizon's shore.
In the gloom, a promise of grace,
Restless glimmers, a warm embrace.

Then let them dance, these fragments of light,
In the overcast, they burn so bright.
For even in shadows, we find our way,
Restless glimmers guiding the day.

Enigmatic Pearls in a Sea of Night

In the velvet dark, secrets reside,
Enigmatic pearls in quiet tide.
Swaying softly in moonlit dreams,
Glistening softly with silvery gleams.

Each pearl a mystery, deep and wide,
Holding whispers the stars confide.
Within the depths, they shimmer and swirl,
Fragments of stories in a cosmic whirl.

Floating softly on waves of time,
Echoes of laughter intertwine.
In the sea of night, they drift and gleam,
Enigmatic pearls, lost in a dream.

Each wave, a heartbeat, each tide, a sigh,
In their embrace, we learn to fly.
Boundless horizons of darkness and light,
Enigmatic pearls guide us through night.

So dive into the depths, be unafraid,
For pearls are found where shadows wade.
In the sea of night, our souls unite,
Enigmatic pearls, forever alight.

Celestial Sorrow Within the Night's Grasp

In the shadows of the moon,
Whispers linger, soft and soon.
Tears like dew on petals rest,
Hearts entwined, forever pressed.

Midnight sighs in heavy tones,
Stars above like ancient stones.
A tapestry of dreams laid bare,
Within the night, a silent prayer.

Time stands still beneath her gaze,
Fractured smiles through endless haze.
Echoes haunt the quiet hours,
Moonlit paths adorned with flowers.

Lonely breezes softly wail,
Carrying each sorrowed tale.
Galaxies with hearts of glass,
Twinkle softly as they pass.

Yet in sorrow, beauty glows,
As the night in silence grows.
In every tear, a light does spark,
Celestial sorrows in the dark.

Fleeting Glows amid a Misty Memory

Fleeting lights in shadows dance,
Memory calls, a soft romance.
Echoes of a fleeting past,
Mist drapes softly, spells are cast.

Glimmers fade with morning's rise,
Hidden truths behind the skies.
Whispers linger, soft and low,
In the heart, the shadows grow.

Through the haze, a vision stands,
Time entwined in gentle hands.
Moments caught like fireflies,
Fleeting glows that mesmerize.

In the twilight, dreams arise,
Caught between all truth and lies.
Memory's touch is bittersweet,
Every pulse a fast retreat.

Yet in the mist, the heart shall know,
Fleeting glows still softly show.
A dance of light on twilight streams,
Amidst a sea of faded dreams.

The Vesper's Lament in a Glistening Hub

The vesper sings a soft lament,
In the night, the stars are spent.
Glistening dreams like dew arise,
In every heart, a hidden prize.

Whispers echo where shadows tread,
In the hub where silence bled.
Evening's breath paints skies in blue,
A canvas bright where hopes break through.

Time will weave a tale so vast,
Memories held, but not to last.
Each heartbeat like a distant drum,
In the twinkle, lost loves hum.

Amidst the glow, a sigh persists,
In the dark, the moonlight twists.
The vesper's song, a mournful call,
In this hub, we rise and fall.

Yet in the lament, strength shall grow,
Through the trials that we know.
In every tear, a pathway found,
In the glistening, hope unbound.

Softly Shining in the Starlit Abyss

In the vastness, stars align,
Softly shining, pure and fine.
Each glow a tale from far away,
In the night, their secrets stay.

A gentle breeze with velvet grace,
Caresses time in endless space.
In the starlit, shadows play,
Dancing lightly, drift away.

Whispers float on cosmic winds,
Journey where the silence begins.
Every twinkle, a wish reborn,
Softly shining, never worn.

Across the depths, our dreams still roam,
Finding light to guide us home.
In the abyss, despair takes flight,
With each star, reignites the night.

So let us wander, hand in hand,
In the starlit dreams so grand.
Together we'll break through the night,
Softly shining, hearts alight.

Shattered Reflections of Fantasy

Dreams splinter like glass at dawn,
Visions dance on rippling streams.
Fleeting moments now withdrawn,
Echoes lost in silent screams.

Faint whispers of what could be,
Fragments trapped in time's embrace.
Shadows weave in mystery,
Fantasies we dare not chase.

With each glimmer, hope takes flight,
Yet the shards wound deep inside.
In the chaos, seek the light,
Where shattered dreams may still abide.

Mirror worlds that twirl and spin,
Reflecting laughter, joy, and tears.
In the void, where dreams begin,
We wander through our deepest fears.

With every cut, a tale is spun,
Sparks ignite within the night.
From broken dreams, new paths are won,
In shattered realms, we find our might.

When the Stars Weep Glittering Tears

In the velvet cloak of night,
Stars weep drops of silver light.
Each tear glimmers, full of dreams,
Carrying tales through moonlit beams.

Whispers float on cosmic winds,
Secrets laden, time rescinds.
Galaxies dance in waltz so grand,
As sorrows etch on the darkened land.

Stillness holds the breath of space,
Twinkling voices, a soft embrace.
In the quiet, we find our fears,
When the stars weep glittering tears.

Each drop a wish, a prayer set free,
Floating down like petals from a tree.
As they land, they gently hum,
Songs of hope, where love is from.

We look above, hearts interlace,
In the tears, we find our place.
With starlit dreams, we shall ascend,
When the cosmos chooses to mend.

Glows of Remorse in Twilight's Breath

Twilight falls with muted grace,
Casting shadows on a wistful face.
In soft hues of fading light,
Regrets linger, haunting the night.

Every glow tells tales of yore,
Whispers echo from the shore.
Memories dance like fleeting ghosts,
In the stillness, that which boasts.

Caught between what was and will,
Twilight's breath, a sacred thrill.
With each pulse, a heartache churns,
As the sun's final ember burns.

Remorse shimmers in twilight's glow,
A fleeting touch, a gentle woe.
In the dusk, we face our truths,
In every sigh, a hint of youth.

In the twilight's tender embrace,
We learn to find our rightful place.
Through glows of remorse, we mend,
In twilight's breath, we make amends.

Secrets Encased in Shiny Veils

Wrapped in layers, secrets hide,
Encased in veils, where fears abide.
Glistening fabric, soft and bright,
Holds whispered truths far from sight.

With every fold, a story's told,
Of dreams anew and hearts grown cold.
Shiny shields, they mask the pain,
As we dance in our own chain.

In shadows deep, we long to break,
To touch the light, to feel awake.
Yet behind the veil, we stay concealed,
Unraveled truths remain unrevealed.

As layers part, the air grows still,
In the quiet, we seek our will.
Beneath the glimmer, hearts reside,
Secrets encased, a tender guide.

We chase the dawn, through veils we weave,
In the shiny depths, we learn to grieve.
From every thread, we find our way,
To shed the fears that meant to stay.

Lament of a Glistening Tear

In shadows deep, a tear does fall,
A silent whisper, a muted call.
It glistens bright, yet hides its pain,
A story weaved in loss and gain.

Each drop that falls, a memory lost,
In hidden depths, it's time that costs.
A fragile heart bears all its weight,
Yet in the night, it finds its fate.

Through sorrow's path, the tear will weave,
A silver thread, a heart that grieves.
Yet in that glint, a spark of hope,
To climb again, to learn to cope.

As dawn draws near, the tear will glow,
Reflecting life, the ebb and flow.
From grief's embrace, the spirit flies,
To rise anew beneath the skies.

For every tear that glistens bright,
Is but a step towards the light.
In laments soft, we find our way,
To heal the heart at break of day.

Twilight's Veil on Faery Wings

In twilight hush, the faeries dance,
With whispers soft, they take their chance.
On gossamer wings, they weave the night,
A magic spell, a lovely sight.

Among the blooms, they softly glide,
In shimmering veils, they seek to hide.
Their laughter twinkles, sweet and light,
As stars awaken, bidding night.

Through silver beams, their circuits flow,
Casting dreams in a gentle glow.
A world unseen, yet ever near,
In dusk's embrace, they disappear.

With every flutter, stories spun,
Of ancient tales and battles won.
In twilight's veil, the heart takes flight,
On faery wings, through endless night.

So listen close when night is still,
For faery magic can fulfill.
In whispers soft, let dreams take wing,
In twilight's hush, the faeries sing.

A Flickering Heartbeat in the Dark

In silence deep, a heartbeat flows,
A flicker bright where shadows grow.
It pulses soft against the night,
A fragile flame, a fleeting light.

With every thrum, a secret speaks,
In darkened depths where solace seeks.
A rhythm slow, yet strong and true,
A dance of hope that breaks on through.

When stars do fade and shadows creep,
A flickering light begins to leap.
Though darkness wraps with cold embrace,
The heartbeat finds its sacred space.

Amidst despair, it whispers clear,
Against the void, it conquers fear.
A flickering spark within the gloom,
Awakening life, dispelling doom.

So let it beat, this heart of fire,
In darkest times, it lifts us higher.
With every pulse, we rise anew,
A beacon bright, forever true.

The Enigma of Little Lost Orbs

In twilight's hue, little orbs stray,
Each one a wish that faded away.
They glint like stars in a restless sea,
Holding secrets of what could be.

Once bright with dreams, now draped in night,
They twirl in silence, devoid of light.
With every turn, a story lost,
Of innocence born, yet never embossed.

These little orbs, they wander far,
A dance of shadows, a ghostly spar.
In circles round, they search for grace,
Longing for hands to find their place.

But in their flight, the heart will sigh,
For dreams once held now choose to fly.
Yet still they shimmer, a hopeful tone,
A testament to the dreams we've known.

So gaze with wonder at these lost lights,
With faith we gather what ignites.
In every flicker, a promise stays,
That dreams reborn will find their ways.

Serene Cinders Beneath the Moon

In twilight's hush, the embers glow,
Soft whispers dance where shadows flow.
A tranquil heart, in night's embrace,
Finds solace in the night's sweet grace.

Dreams flicker like the waning light,
As stars unveil their gleaming sight.
In stillness, thoughts like rivers roam,
The mind transcends to realms called home.

Beneath the moon, our troubles cease,
In silent nights, we seek our peace.
With every breath, the world feels new,
As cinders glow, our spirits flu.

Through echoes of the past we tread,
On paths where timeless tales are read.
The night will hush our whispered fears,
As serenity wipes away the tears.

Together near the glowing pyre,
We forge our hopes, ignite the fire.
The cinders spark with endless dreams,
In moonlit glow, life's beauty beams.

Hidden Luminance Beneath the Veil

In whispers soft, the veils do part,
Revealing wonders that warm the heart.
A dance of light in shadow's clutch,
Hides secrets that we crave so much.

Beneath the layers, colors blend,
Where magic waits, around each bend.
A luminous pulse, unseen, it glows,
In every nook, where hope bestows.

With gentle hands, we lift the shroud,
To find the spark, yet unavowed.
A flicker stirs, ignites the night,
Unraveling truths wrapped up in light.

Through fragile forms, our visions glide,
In luminescence, fears subside.
Hidden gems, like stars, align,
As shadows dance with dreams divine.

From depths of dusk, a glow will rise,
The veil will lift, to clear our skies.
In every heartbeat, there's a sign,
That hidden light will soon be mine.

Murmurs of Spectral Desires

Through muted paths where shadows blend,
A haunting whisper knows no end.
Desires flicker, ethereal hue,
In spectral forms, they call to you.

As twilight draws its curtain close,
The echoes weave a fragrant prose.
With every sigh, a dream takes flight,
In murmurs soft, we chase the night.

A gentle breath, a shiver's trace,
The night unveils its hidden grace.
With spectral wings, our wishes soar,
To realms where yearnings dance and explore.

In shadows deep, our hearts do seek,
The whispered truths that dare to speak.
For in the darkness, spark ignites,
And every dream begets new sights.

In spectral lights of varying shades,
The longing lingers, never fades.
With every pulse, the night inspires,
As dreams converge, with murmurs' desires.

When Light Dims in the Faded Realm

When twilight cloaks the day in gray,
The fading light begins to sway.
In silent tones, the shadows blend,
As dusk prepares, our thoughts descend.

The world grows hushed, yet echoes call,
In this dim space, we feel it all.
Each fleeting spark, a fleeting trace,
Of memories lost, yet we embrace.

In corners where the whispers hide,
Unraveled hopes no longer bide.
A gentle dimness, soothing balm,
In faded realms, we find our calm.

With every breath, the stillness reigns,
While fleeting light speaks of our pains.
In depths of dusk, we learn to feel,
The beauty found in shadows' seal.

As dreams dissolve in twilight's fold,
We gather strength, more brave than bold.
For when the light dims, we ignite,
A flicker bright, reclaiming night.

Ethereal Flickers in a Dusk Garden

Whispers of evening dance in the air,
Petals of twilight, fragrant and rare.
Stars begin to peek through the haze,
A symphony of crickets softly plays.

Shadows stretch long, embracing the night,
Moonlight spills silver, gentle and bright.
Fireflies flit like wishes set free,
Guiding lost dreams to the heart of the tree.

Breezes carry secrets of days gone by,
Echoes of laughter beneath the sky.
In this enchanted, tranquil retreat,
The essence of magic makes all hearts beat.

Night-blooming flowers unfold with grace,
Casting their spells in this sacred space.
Moments enshrined in the fading light,
Where memories linger, cherished and bright.

As dusk weaves its fabric, soft and profound,
The garden breathes life, a comforting sound.
Ethereal flickers, both fleeting and grand,
In the dusk garden, where dreams take a stand.

Lost Lanterns in the Realm of Fables

In a forest thick with stories untold,
Flickering lanterns twinkle like gold.
Paths entwine with whispers of lore,
Each step revealing what dreams have in store.

Beneath ancient branches, shadows conspire,
Tales of the brave, tales of desire.
Magic and mystery lace every breath,
As dusk descends, embracing the depth.

Lost wanderers seek their guiding light,
In the realm of fables, bold and bright.
Footprints forgotten on time's dusty way,
Yearning for solace, to find where they stay.

Through flickering flames, a story unfolds,
Of journeys taken, of treasures and gold.
The heart of the forest beats deep and wide,
With lost lanterns glowing, where dreams reside.

In night's gentle hold, magic finds its place,
Every lost lantern a forgotten face.
Embrace the enchantment, let it take flight,
In the realm of fables, lost in the night.

Melancholy Gems in the Underworld of Wonders

Deep in the darkness, where shadows emerge,
Lie gems of sorrow, a haunting surge.
Reflecting the dreams that were left behind,
In the underworld's heart, a soul intertwined.

Whispers echo softly, a lullaby's plea,
Cradled in twilight, before twilight flees.
Embers of hope flicker dim but bright,
Guiding the weary through velvet night.

In chambers of silence, echoes take flight,
Melancholy gems, shining with light.
Each facet a story, a tear softly shed,
In the embrace of wonders, where lost hopes tread.

Among shadows and dreams, new paths will grow,
Wonders bloom softly, where sorrows flow.
Sunkissed reflections in the depths of despair,
Reveal the beauty in what lingers there.

The underworld glimmers, a tapestry spun,
With threads of emotion, where all is begun.
Melancholy gems, they whisper and sing,
In the arms of the night, a bittersweet ring.

Faded Radiance of Elfin Sorrows

In a glade where the twilight weaves grace,
Elfin sorrows linger, soft as lace.
Faded radiance glimmers through tears,
A tapestry woven of dreams and fears.

Moonbeams cascade on delicate wings,
Where once there was laughter, now silence clings.
The echoes of magic twist through the night,
Illuminating shadows; fading from sight.

Glimmers of joy in the gardens of pain,
A fleeting remembrance of sunshine and rain.
Each sigh of the night carries tales of the past,
In soft, whispered tones, in a world unsurpassed.

As starlight dwindles, elfin hearts ache,
The rivers of time, they bend and they break.
In the silence of dusk, their shadows take flight,
Embracing the weariness of fading light.

A dance of the bittersweet shadows remains,
In the heart of the glade, where the longing sustains.
Faded radiance lingers, a touch of the divine,
In the elfin sorrows, where love will entwine.

Lost Glimmers in an Urban Maze

Neon shadows dance and sway,
Beneath the city's tireless hum.
Whispers of dreams fade away,
In this labyrinth we succumb.

Brick and glass rise to the sky,
Echoes of footsteps linger near.
Stars blink softly, wondering why,
Hope feels distant, cloaked in fear.

A flicker in the alleyway,
A sigh, a glance from afar.
Lost glimmers beckon our stay,
Yet guide us back to the scar.

Across the corners we will roam,
Seeking light in every turn.
The asphalt heart, a weary home,
In its pulse, our dreams still yearn.

Hold onto what we cannot touch,
Breathe in the quiet, don't forget.
In this maze, it matters much,
Every lost glimmer is a debt.

The Frayed Ends of Celestial Threads

Stars unravel in the night,
Stitching dreams with golden thread.
A universe lost to sight,
Whispers of worlds that we dread.

Galaxies wane, softly fade,
Lost among the vast unknown.
The fabric of night's parade,
Holds stories of seeds once sown.

Tangled thoughts in cosmic lace,
Each woven strand tells a tale.
The brilliance of time and space,
Yet, within, shadows prevail.

Celestial echoes fall apart,
As constellations bow and weep.
In this tapestry, a heart,
Each frayed end, secrets to keep.

The night sky weeps, yet still glows,
For even in darkness, there's grace.
Within the frayed, a truth flows,
A connection time can't erase.

The Iridescence of Melancholy

A tear like glass reflects the light,
In colors strange and deep as night.
Melancholy sings its song,
In hues that feel both right and wrong.

Unraveled thoughts in tender grace,
Each whisper seems to leave a trace.
A chill that dances on the skin,
Where shadows blur, the light begins.

Iridescent dreams unfold,
Within the stillness of the cold.
Layers of sorrow intertwine,
Yet, beauty rises with each line.

Among the echoes, we will dwell,
In bittersweetness, find our cell.
The depth of sadness, rich and whole,
Breathes life anew into the soul.

In every shade, a story spun,
A tapestry of what's begun.
In the iridescence we may find,
The joy that lingers, intertwined.

Hues of Silence in a Twilight Heart

Twilight cloaks the waking world,
In violet whispers softly swirled.
Each moment heavy with the weight,
Of silence that begins to sate.

Shadows stretch and softly creep,
Across the edges where we sleep.
A pulse beneath the fading light,
Marks the end of day's delight.

In stillness, colors drift and blend,
The heart beats slow, it seeks to mend.
Hues of silence paint the air,
Each breath a secret, born of care.

Beneath the stars, a silence grows,
In the twilight, hope softly glows.
Every shade a tender sigh,
Echoing dreams that linger high.

Hold dear the quiet, hear the call,
In the twilight's arms, we find it all.
For in the hush of nature's art,
We discover hues of the heart.

Fragile Hues in a Dreamer's Snare

In twilight's grasp, soft whispers play,
Colors dance in a delicate array.
A canvas woven with threads of night,
Dreamers linger in fading light.

Chasing shadows that linger and fade,
Lost in visions that softly cascade.
Each hue a secret, each shade a sigh,
Fragile dreams that flutter and fly.

Beneath the stars, where silence hums,
Canvas of silence, where longing drums.
The heart beats gently, to visions it flees,
In fragile hues, the soul finds ease.

Eclipsed by night, yet hope still gleams,
Reflected in the fabric of our dreams.
A symphony of colors, tender and rare,
Forever tangled in a dreamer's snare.

Awake at dawn, the moment is gone,
Yet echoes linger like a soft, warm song.
In life's palette, bright futures bloom,
Transforming shadows into light's sweet room.

Chimeric Glows of Forgotten Lore

In ancient woods where whispers weave,
Chimeric glows of tales that grieve.
Each tree a sentinel, secrets it holds,
In bark and bough, the past unfolds.

Luminous shadows dance on the ground,
In every flicker, lost dreams are found.
The air is thick with a timeworn sigh,
Echoes of laughter that flutter and die.

Beneath the moon, where stars confess,
Legends sleep in a soft caress.
Forgotten lore on the wind does sway,
Guiding the souls who've lost their way.

Fables twine in the rustling leaves,
Stories hidden, each heart believes.
With chimeric glows, they softly implore,
To remember the tales that we adore.

As dawn approaches, the visions fade,
Yet in our hearts, the magic is laid.
Forever woven in time's gentle shore,
Chimeric glows of forgotten lore.

Fablestitch of Light and Shadow

In the weave of fate, threads intertwine,
Fables are stitched with design divine.
Light and shadow, a dance so sweet,
Together they form the heartbeat's beat.

On fabric spun from the dreams we weave,
Stories unfold, we dare to believe.
Each stitch a moment, a tale graced,
In the loom of time, our lives are traced.

Illuminated paths where shadows play,
Echoes of laughter chase sorrows away.
In golden glimmers and twilight's veil,
The tapestry whispers a timeless tale.

With every thread, a memory shines,
In the art of life, where love aligns.
A fablestitch binding dark and bright,
In harmony's grasp, both wrong and right.

From the quiet corners where dreams reside,
To vibrant realms where the heart is tied.
In the dance of light, we're never alone,
Fablestitch tales, in love we've grown.

Celestial Lament from a Hidden Heart

Stars weep softly in the vast expanse,
A celestial lament in twilight's dance.
Whispers of cosmos twirl in sighs,
As secrets tremble in night's dark eyes.

Beneath the shimmer, a longing burns,
For dreams unspoken, the heart yearns.
Each twinkle a memory, a story to tell,
In the silence of space where shadows dwell.

Galaxies spin with elegance profound,
Yet in their beauty, the lost are found.
Hearts hidden beneath the infinite sky,
In celestial songs that rise and fly.

A moonlit sigh, a comet's trail,
In every whisper, the hopes unveil.
The pulse of the cosmos, a haunting art,
Resonates deeply from a hidden heart.

As dawn approaches, the stars grow faint,
But their soft lament, a soothing paint.
In every heartbeat, our spirits take flight,
With celestial love, through the still of night.

Celestial Tears on a Moonlit String

Soft whispers fall from stars above,
Dancing gently on the silver night.
Each teardrop glistens with sweet love,
Eclipsing shadows with pure light.

Faint echoes linger in the air,
Mingling dreams and midnight sighs.
Cradled softly in a lover's care,
Beneath the watchful, wistful skies.

Moonbeams weave through branches bare,
Creating tapestries of grace.
A symphony of silence rare,
In the calm, a tender embrace.

Notes of sorrow blend with glee,
As the night sings its sweet refrain.
In this realm, we are truly free,
Bound by love, not by the pain.

Celestial tears on strings of night,
Guide the heart through darkened streams.
A melody of purest light,
A serenade for whispered dreams.

Fragments of Light in the Enchanted Veil

In the depths of twilight's glow,
Fragments dance upon the breeze.
Scattered echoes, soft and slow,
Woven through the ancient trees.

Glimmers form a tapestry,
Of the stories left untold.
Whispers weave a mystery,
In the night, the truth unfolds.

Veils of silver, threads of gold,
Illuminate the shadowed path.
Every glint, a tale of old,
Lost in time's relentless wrath.

Where the stars and wishes meet,
Hope ignites in every heart.
A serenade both soft and sweet,
As life's wonders play their part.

Fragments glisten in the dark,
A mosaic of dreams and fears.
In the stillness, love will spark,
Guided by the light of years.

Sorrowful Glimmers Beneath Enchantment

Beneath the veil of twilight dim,
Lies a world of whispered sighs.
Sorrowful glimmers dwell within,
As the night embraces cries.

Stars weep gently, lost in thought,
As moonlit shadows roam the ground.
Each forgotten wish and naught,
Echo in silence profound.

The forest breathes a heavy tune,
Carrying echoes of the past.
Every heart that breaks too soon,
Lingers in the night's contrast.

Amidst the darkness, hope takes flight,
Cloaked in the shimmer of despair.
Yet in the depths of endless night,
Beauty whispers softly there.

Glimmers glisten, bittersweet,
In the charmed embrace of fate.
Sorrow finds a way to meet,
Enchantment woven, love innate.

The Lament of Glittering Phantoms

In the twilight, phantoms sigh,
Drifting softly through the mist.
Glittering shadows float on high,
As lost dreams become a tryst.

Echoes whisper tales of yore,
Fractured memories take their flight.
Each lament an haunting score,
Fading gently into night.

Stars ignite with longing's flame,
Guiding souls through midnight's maze.
Yet each spark holds grief a name,
Caught in the web of time's gaze.

Phantoms dance on silver streams,
With every whirl a silent tear.
In the space between the dreams,
Hope and heartache intertwine near.

A lament for the lost and found,
In the embrace of twilight's breath.
Glittering phantoms spin around,
In the shadows of life and death.

Whispers of the Glowing Abyss

In shadows deep, a voice does rise,
Eclipsed by light, beneath the skies.
Whispers dance on the ocean's swell,
Secrets held where dark dreams dwell.

Stars reflect on water's face,
Guiding hearts to a sacred place.
Echoes linger, soft and clear,
In the abyss, we shed our fear.

With every breath, the night unfolds,
Tales of wonder, yet untold.
A shimmering path, we dare to tread,
In the glowing depths, where souls are led.

Beneath the moon, the currents sway,
Drawing us to where shadows play.
A melody that calls us home,
In the abyss where we freely roam.

To the whispers, we must heed,
In the dark, our spirits freed.
In silence deep, truth shall appear,
In the glowing abyss, we lose our fear.

Celestial Gloom in a Luminous Whisper

Beneath the stars, a quiet sigh,
In celestial gloom, dreams fly high.
Whispers weave through the fabric tight,
Casting shadows that dance with light.

Glowing embers in the still of night,
A tapestry of lover's flight.
In the stillness, hearts intertwine,
Embracing moments, forever divine.

Through the void, a shimmer glows,
Guiding lost souls, gently it flows.
In the velvet dark, we pause to see,
A luminous whisper, our destiny.

Stars reflect on the waters deep,
In meaning hidden, secrets keep.
With gentle hands, the night unfolds,
In celestial dreams, our fate is told.

Underneath the silvered skies,
Life's quiet truths begin to rise.
In luminous whispers, we find our way,
Celestial gloom beckons to stay.

Timeless Flickers Amidst the Forgotten

In twilight's grasp, a soft glow gleams,
Flickers of hope, forgotten dreams.
A fragile light, where shadows reign,
Guides the lost through whispered pain.

Amidst the ruins, life tries to breathe,
With timeless flickers, hearts believe.
Each spark a story, rich and vast,
Connecting the future with echoes past.

Through darkened halls, the light will rise,
Bold and brave, beneath the skies.
In the silence, we heed the call,
Timeless flickers will not fall.

In every ember, a promise held,
In the darkest depths, stories swelled.
They dance and twirl, in stark insistence,
Against the tide, with fierce persistence.

Lost allies' faces in the glow,
Guide us forth where the shadows flow.
Together we face what fate has spun,
Timeless flickers, we are not done.

The Elegy of Fading Illumination

In a world where bright lights fade,
An elegy sings, softly conveyed.
Memories flicker, like stars in flight,
Whispering tales of lost delight.

Silhouettes dance on the walls of time,
Each moment cherished, lost in rhyme.
The echoes of laughter, once so bright,
Now linger softly, a hush of night.

As shadows stretch from dusk to dawn,
Fading illumination carries on.
In every heartbeat, a longing stays,
For the brilliance of those golden days.

From twilight's arms, we bid farewell,
To moments captured in a fragile shell.
Yet in the dark, our spirits fight,
Holding onto dreams, igniting light.

The elegy whispers of what's lost,
Yet in our hearts, we bear the cost.
For even as the bright lights wane,
Fading illumination leaves its stain.

www.ingramcontent.com/pod-product-compliance
Ingram Content Group UK Ltd.
Pitfield, Milton Keynes, MK11 3LW, UK
UKHW021434160125
4146UKWH00006B/84